CHRISTMAS

A selection of bad taste cartoons
from the Silvey–Jex Partnership

FIRST PRINTED IN ENGLAND BY MERLIN COLOUR PRINTERS. CANVEY ISLAND.
ISBN 0 907280 08 0

"Not today thank you."

"Well, it looks like a pile of reindeer droppings to me."

"...Two kings and a spade."

"If it's there . . . he'll step in it."

"You're not Father Christmas."

"Look Barabbas – a little friend for you."

"Down Donder, down Dancer, down Dasher, down Blitzen..."

"That makes fifteen 'Congratulations on your new arrival' and one 'Merry Christmas.'"

"Alright – alright – I'll be up in a minute."

"Well somebody's got to go"

"Well . . . you said there was no such person . . . now there isn't."

"Places everyone . . . here they come."

"Bah Humbug."

"Ho! Ho! Ho!"

"That was some thaw!"

"Got a nice bit of venison today sir."